MACMILLAN READERS

BEGINNER LEVEL

HERMAN MELVILLE

Billy Budd

Retold by Margaret Tarner

GW00455769

MACMILLAN

30130 140472357

BEGINNER LEVEL

Founding Editor: John Milne

The Macmillan Readers provide a choice of enjoyable reading materials for learners of English. The series is published at six levels – Starter, Beginner, Elementary, Pre-intermediate, Intermediate and Upper.

Level control
Information, structure and vocabulary are controlled to suit the students' ability at each level.

The number of words at each level:

Starter	about 300 basic words
Beginner	about 600 basic words
Elementary	about 1100 basic words
Pre-intermediate	about 1400 basic words
Intermediate	about 1600 basic words
Upper	about 2200 basic words

Vocabulary
Some difficult words and phrases in this book are important for understanding the story. Some of these words are explained in the story and some are shown in the pictures. From Pre-intermediate level upwards, words are marked with a number like this: …³. These words are explained in the Glossary at the end of the book.

Contents

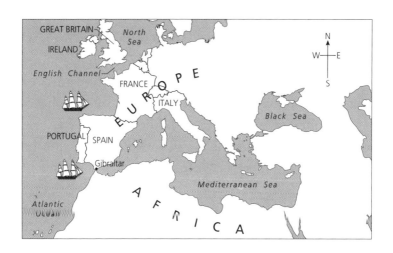

A Note About the Author

Herman Melville was an American. He was born on 1st August 1819, in New York City. From the age of fifteen, Herman Melville had many different jobs. He worked in a bank. He worked on ships. He was a teacher in a school.

In 1841, Melville worked on a ship called *Acushnet*. It sailed to the Pacific Ocean. The sailors on the *Acushnet* hunted whales and killed them. After many adventures in the Pacific islands, Melville sailed on a ship called *The United States*. This ship belonged to the US Navy.

In 1844, Melville left the US Navy. He began to write stories. These stories were about sailors, ships and the islands in the Pacific Ocean. These stories were popular.

In 1847, Herman married Elizabeth Shaw. Three years later, they bought a farm in the state of Massachusetts. They had two sons and one daughter.

Melville travelled to the Middle East in 1857. He wrote more books and he began to write poetry. But he was no longer a popular writer. He had to sell some of his land.

After the American Civil War in 1863, Melville went back to New York City. He worked in a government office. He lived in New York City until he died. He died on 28th September 1891. He was 72 years old.

Some of Herman Melville's stories are: *Typee* (1846), *Omoo* (1847), *Mardi* (1849), *Redburn* (1849), *White-jacket* (1850) and his famous story about a whale – *Moby Dick* (1851). *Billy Budd* was Melville's last story. It was published in 1924, 33 years after Melville's death.

A Note About This Story

Time: 1797. **Place:** the Mediterranean Sea.

This was a time of wars and revolutions. Many people did not want kings to rule their countries anymore. The people wanted more food, better work and more freedom.

In 1797, George III was King of Great Britain and Ireland. There was a war between France and Britain. The French and British armies fought battles on the land. The French and British navies fought battles on the sea.

Warships were made of wood. They had many sails and huge, powerful guns. (Look at pages 6 and 7.) Each warship had hundreds of men on board. Some of the men were sailors. Some of the men were officers. The sailors cooked the food and they cleaned the ship. They listened to the orders from the officers. Then the sailors steered the ship. They moved the sails. The sails made the ship go faster or slower. Some of the sailors fired the huge guns. They were the gunners.

There were also marines and corporals on warships. Marines were special soldiers. They fought in battles at sea.

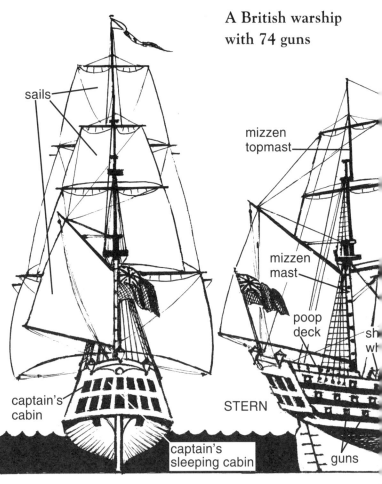

A British warship with 74 guns

sails

mizzen topmast

mizzen mast

poop deck

sh
wl

captain's cabin

STERN

captain's sleeping cabin

guns

gunners

gun

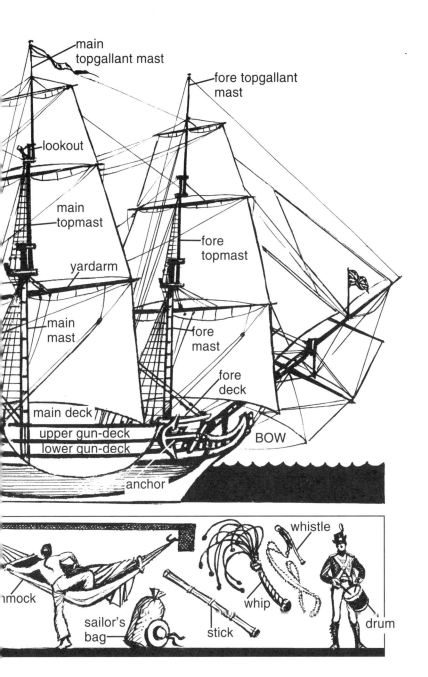

main topgallant mast

fore topgallant mast

lookout

main topmast

fore topmast

yardarm

main mast

fore mast

fore deck

main deck

upper gun-deck

lower gun-deck

BOW

anchor

hammock

sailor's bag

stick

whip

whistle

drum

7

Corporals were the policemen on the ship. The master-at-arms was in charge of the corporals. All these men lived together on the ship for many months.

At this time, sailors lived in bad conditions. They were often cold and wet. They were paid very little money. Their food was bad. Their work was dangerous and hard. Sea battles were frightening and terrible and very many sailors died in battles. Many more got horrible injuries.

In the eighteenth century, the British Navy needed many sailors for the warships. Sailors were often impressed. Officers went to towns or onto trading-ships. They beat the sailors and took them to the warships. These impressed men had to stay on the warships. They had to work and they had to fight. Some of them never saw their homes or their families again.

In Spring 1797, some sailors in the British Navy mutinied. They did not want to work. They did not want to fight. They wanted more money and better conditions. They wanted the impressing to stop. The admirals of the navy were very worried. Britain and France were at war. Mutiny was treason. The sailors were making trouble for their country. They were helping France, the enemy of Britain.

Admiral Nelson was an important officer in the British Navy. He was a brave man and a good officer. He spoke to the other admirals. After that, the navy made better conditions for the British sailors.

The People in This Story

Captain Edward Vere
ˈkæptɪn ˈedwʊd vɪə

Lieutenant Ratcliffe
lefˈtenant ˈrætklɪf

William ('Billy') Budd
ˈwɪljʌm (ˈbɪli) bʌd
(a foretopman)

John Claggart
dʒɒn ˈklægət
(the master-at-arms)

Dansker
ˈdænskə
(a sailor)

Squeak
skwiːk
(a gunner)

Albert
ˈælbət
(a servant)

Note: HMS = His Majesty's Ship. 'God Bless You!' = 'God will love you.' *Indomitable*, say ɪnˈdɒmɪtəbl.

1

A British Warship

It was the summer of 1797. Britain and France were at war. The British Navy was fighting the French Navy.

Edward Vere was the captain of a British warship. Captain Vere wanted more sailors for his ship. He did not have enough men to fight battles.

Captain Vere's ship was called *HMS Indomitable*. It had a large crew and it had seventy-four big guns.

There were hundreds of men on *HMS Indomitable*. Every sailor on the ship had a special job. Some of the men were gunners. They fired the huge guns at enemy ships. Some of the men climbed the masts and pulled the ropes. They moved the *Indomitable's* huge sails. Other men were lookouts. They sat at the tops of the tall masts and watched for enemy ships.

The ship's officers blew their whistles and they gave their orders to the sailors. The sailors heard the sound of the whistles and they listened for the officers' orders. The officers were in charge of the sailors. And Edward Vere was in charge of all the officers and sailors on the *Indomitable*.

Captain Vere was a brave man and a good captain. He was kind to the sailors on his ship. But he watched them very carefully.

In the spring of that year – 1797 – there were two mutinies on British warships. Impressed men started the mutinies. The sailors on the warships did not obey their officers' orders. They tried to fight the officers. But the mutinies did not succeed. There were trials. Some of the sailors on the ships had to die.

The mutinies finished quickly. But it had been an unhappy time for the British Navy. And after that spring, all the captains of British warships watched their sailors very carefully. They watched their impressed men most carefully. No captain wanted a mutiny on his ship.

A few of the sailors on *HMS Indomitable* had been in the mutinies. That summer, Captain Vere watched them very carefully. They did not make any trouble.

But Captain Vere was worried. He did not have enough sailors to fight battles. He wanted more men for the *Indomitable*.

2

The Trading-ship

One day, *HMS Indomitable* passed a British trading-ship in the Channel.

The captain called one of his officers.

'Lieutenant Ratcliffe,' said Captain Vere. 'We must have some more men. Sail after that ship. Take some men and a boat. Go on board the ship. Bring some of its men back to the *Indomitable*. They must fight for their king and their country!'

HMS Indomitable stopped the trading-ship. Lieutenant Ratcliffe and some of his sailors got into a small boat. They rowed the boat to the trading-ship and they went on board it.

The ship's captain looked at Ratcliffe and his men. He was not happy.

'What do you want?' he asked.

'Britain is at war, sir!' Ratcliffe answered. 'I must have some of your men. Call your crew onto the deck!'

The captain of the trading-ship obeyed the order. He called his sailors onto the main deck. They stood in a line in front of the lieutenant.

Ratcliffe looked at all the men carefully. Most of them were old, ill and weak. He did not want any of these men. But there was one young man with them. He was strong and handsome. He had bright blue eyes.

'What's your name?' the officer asked the handsome sailor.

'William Budd, sir,' the young man answered. 'People call me Billy Budd, sir.'

Lieutenant Ratcliffe smiled.

'You are young and strong, Billy,' he said. 'I'll take you. I don't want any of the others.'

The captain of the trading-ship was very unhappy.

'You are taking my best man!' he said.

'I'm sorry, Captain,' Ratcliffe replied. 'Billy Budd must fight for his king and his country now. Billy, bring your things. Be quick!'

'Billy is a hard worker,' the captain said sadly. 'He is always happy. And all the men in our crew are happy too. The men don't fight each other any more. And they work hard.'

'Hasn't Billy got any enemies?' Ratcliffe asked.

'No,' the captain replied. 'At first, one man did hate Billy. That man – we called him Redbeard – was very big and strong. He often made trouble. He often fought the other sailors. Everybody was afraid of him.'

'One day, Redbeard called Billy, "Baby Budd",' the captain said. 'Everybody laughed at Billy. Billy was very angry.'

'What did Budd do?' asked Lieutenant Ratcliffe.

'He tried to speak,' the captain replied. 'But he could not say his words clearly. Sometimes, Billy becomes very angry. Then he stutters. He was angry with Redbeard and he tried to speak to him. But he stuttered. "D–d–d–don't laugh at me," he said. He tried to say some more words, but he couldn't speak any more.'

'Then Billy hit Redbeard,' the captain said.

'Billy couldn't speak,' the captain said. 'So he hit the man, again and again. His hands became his voice!'

'What happened then?' Lieutenant Ratcliffe asked.
'Redbeard fell on the deck,' the captain replied.
'Then Billy smiled at Redbeard and shook his hand,' the captain said. 'After that, he and Redbeard became friends. Nobody laughed at Billy again. But Redbeard didn't make trouble again. Everybody on the ship was happy. There were no more fights. Billy brought peace to the ship.'

At that moment, Billy Budd returned to the main deck of the trading-ship. He was carrying a bag. All his things were in it.

'Here I am, sir,' he said to Ratcliffe. Then he smiled at all his friends. 'Goodbye, happy ship! Goodbye, happy crew!' he said. 'I must fight for my king and my country!'

'Silence, Budd!' Lieutenant Ratcliffe said angrily. 'You are a sailor on a warship now!'

'Billy Budd doesn't want to be an impressed sailor,' Ratcliffe thought. 'Will he make trouble on the *Indomitable?*'

But Ratcliffe was wrong. Billy Budd was happy. He had been happy on the trading-ship. But he wanted to be happy on the warship too.

The two men got into the small boat. Billy laughed. He waved his hand at his friends. Sadly, the crew of the trading-ship waved at him. Billy was going to his new home. He was going to *HMS Indomitable!*

3

Billy Budd, Foretopman

Captain Vere saw Billy Budd and Lieutenant Ratcliffe coming on board HMS *Indomitable*. The captain was not happy.

'Only one man!' he said to himself. 'We must have more sailors.'

But then he looked at the young man, and he smiled. He spoke to Billy.

'You are young and strong,' he said.

'His name is William Budd, sir,' Ratcliffe said.

'Well, William Budd, you will be a foretopman on this ship,' said Captain Vere. 'Do you understand the work of a foretopman?'

Billy looked up at the *Indomitable's* tall fore mast.

'Yes sir,' he replied. 'I will do my best for you, Captain.'

So Billy Budd became a foretopman on HMS *Indomitable*.

All the *Indomitable*'s foretopmen were young and strong. They worked on the ship's tall fore mast. They pulled the ropes and moved the huge sails. Sometimes, they worked near the deck. Sometimes, they worked high on the mast. The foretopmen were lookouts too – that was part of their work. One of the foretopmen was always at the top of the mast. He was watching for enemy ships.

Billy was happy on the foremast. The foretopmen were the best sailors on the *Indomitable*. They were his friends. They were happy too.

But some of the impressed men on the warship were not happy. They wanted to go home. They wanted to see their families.

One day, Lieutenant Ratcliffe spoke to Billy Budd.

'Where is your family, Billy?' he asked.

'I don't know, sir,' Billy replied.

'You don't know?' said Ratcliffe. 'Who was your father?'

'God knows that, sir!' Billy said. And he smiled.

The lieutenant was very surprised.

'Do you know *anything* about your family?' he asked.

'No, sir,' said Billy. 'A good man found me outside his house in Bristol. I was in a little basket and I was wearing fine silk clothes. There was no message in the basket. The good man took me into his house. He took care of me. He gave me my name.'

'A little basket and silk clothes?' said Ratcliffe. 'Your mother came from a rich family, Billy. Well, your mother didn't want you. And your father didn't want you. But we want you Billy! You are a good sailor and a good worker, Billy Budd!'

4
The Master-at-Arms

It was the month of August. *HMS Indomitable* had left the Channel. The warship was now sailing in the Mediterranean Sea, between Spain and Africa.

Captain Vere watched his crew carefully, but there was no trouble on the *Indomitable*. Another man was watching the crew too. His name was John Claggart. He was the master-at-arms. Claggart was a powerful man and a dangerous man.

The master-at-arms was the chief policeman on the *Indomitable*. He was in charge of the ship's policemen – the corporals. Nobody on the *Indomitable* liked John Claggart.

'Who is he? Where did he come from?' the crew asked each other. They did not know the answers to these questions. But they told many stories about the master-at-arms.

He's not an Englishman. He's an American.

No! He isn't an American. He's a Frenchman!

A third man had a different idea.

'Claggart has been in prison,' he said. 'He escaped from prison. Now he's on board this warship. He's safe here. Nobody can punish him here. He punishes *us*!'

Claggart heard all these stories. He did not worry about them. He said nothing. He listened and he smiled. Claggart was clever. And he was a good sailor. But he was not a good man. He was a wicked man.

The master-at-arms was a very cruel man. He always carried a stick. He liked to punish people. He hated the sailors. He wanted them to fight each other. He wanted them to behave badly. He wanted to punish them.

And from Billy Budd's first day on the *Indomitable*, Claggart hated the young sailor. Billy was good and Claggart hated good people. He wanted to punish the young foretopman. But Billy worked hard and he behaved well. He did not want anybody to punish him.

One day, Claggart fell over a young gunner. The young man was running. It was an accident. The man was not trying to hurt Claggart. But Claggart punished the gunner. He gave an order to one of the corporals. The corporal pulled off the young sailor's shirt and beat him with a whip. He beat him very hard.

All the crew had to watch the punishment. Billy saw the red marks on the sailor's back. He was very sorry for the young man.

'I don't want anybody to beat me,' Billy thought. 'I must be very careful. I must never do anything wrong.'

After that, Billy worked harder every day. He tried to do everything right. He obeyed every order quickly. All his friends on the fore mast laughed at him.

But Billy *did* get into trouble.

Sometimes, the young foretopman could not find things. Sometimes his bag was in the wrong place. Sometimes other men's things were in his bag. Sometimes, at night, there was something wrong with Billy's hammock. He could not understand these things. He was very worried.

One of Billy's friends was called Dansker. Dansker was one of the oldest sailors on the *Indomitable*. One day, Billy asked his friend for advice.

'What have I done wrong, Dansker?' Billy asked. 'I don't understand it. Every day, I'm in trouble.'

Dansker smiled. He had sailed on many ships. The old man had sailed on Admiral Nelson's ship, *HMS Agamemnon*. He had fought in many battles. He knew everything about ships and sailors. He understood Billy's problems. He liked the young foretopman and he was sorry for him.

'Billy Budd,' the old sailor said, 'I can answer your question. You have an enemy. And your enemy is Claggart, the master-at-arms. John Claggart hates you, Billy.'

Billy was very surprised.

'The master-at-arms hates me, Dansker?' he said. 'No! You're wrong. He *likes* me. He smiles at me. He is always kind to me.'

'You don't understand Claggart,' Dansker said. 'He likes to punish people. He's a very wicked man. You are good. And Claggart hates good people. And he hates *you*, Billy Budd. John Claggart is a powerful man and a dangerous man. Be careful, Billy. Be careful!'

Billy did not understand his friend's words. But Dansker did not answer any more of his questions.

Billy walked slowly away.

'Does the master-at-arms hate me?' he asked himself. 'No! I don't believe it. I work hard. I like everybody on this ship. And everybody likes me! Dansker is wrong.'

5

The Spy

The next day, another strange thing happened. Billy and some of his friends were eating their midday meal. They were eating hot soup with bread. A strong wind was blowing and there were huge waves on the sea. The *Indomitable* was moving up and down, and from side to side.

Billy and his friends were talking and laughing. Suddenly, a huge wave hit the ship. Billy's soup spilt onto the clean deck.

At that moment, the master-at-arms walked past the men. Billy's soup was on the deck. Claggart stepped over the hot liquid. He did not say anything, but his face was angry. The sailors were frightened. But then the master-at-arms saw Billy and he smiled.

'Ah! Here is Billy Budd!' the master-at-arms said. 'Here is our handsome young sailor! Well done, Billy Budd! Well done!'

The master-at-arms smiled again and he walked on. Billy and his friends saw the smile and they smiled too. Claggart was not angry! All the young sailors laughed. Billy had brought peace to the men of the trading-ship. Had he brought peace to the the men of the *Indomitable* too?

Billy was very happy.

'Dansker was wrong!' he said to himself. 'Mr Claggart likes me.'

But Dansker was not wrong – Billy was wrong. He did not understand the master-at-arms. Claggart's smile was a very cruel smile. It was a terrible smile of hate.

Why did John Claggart, master-at-arms on the *Indomitable*, hate William Budd, foretopman?

Claggart was a wicked man. His mind was full of hate. He had never been happy. He was never going to be happy. He knew that. He hated everyone on the *Indomitable*. And he hated himself.

Wicked people hate everybody. They hate themselves. But most of all, they hate good people. They hate their goodness. The sailors on the warship liked Billy Budd. He was handsome and happy. But most of all, he was good. Why did Claggart hate Billy Budd? He hated Billy's goodness. There was no other reason for his hate.

The master-at-arms was a powerful man. He was the *Indomitable's* chief policemen. He gave orders to the corporals. They watched the sailors. They stopped them fighting. They stopped them talking about the mutinies. The corporals worked for Claggart. Everybody knew about them. But Claggart had other helpers too. Some of the sailors were his spies. They watched the other sailors. They listened to their talk. They told Claggart about their friends.

One of Claggart's spies was called Squeak. He was a gunner. He worked on the upper gun-deck.

One day, Claggart spoke to Squeak.

'Follow William Budd,' Claggart said to Squeak. 'Watch him! Listen to him! Tell me everything about him.'

After that, Squeak followed Billy Budd every day. He watched Billy working. He listened to the young foretopman and his friends. And every day, he spoke to the master-at-arms. He told lies about Billy to Claggart.

'Why did Billy Budd spill his soup in front of you?' Squeak said to Claggart. 'I know the answer, sir. He wanted you to fall on the deck. He wanted to hurt you. And he wanted the crew to laugh at you. Budd calls you bad names, sir. He and his friends laugh at you, sir!'

Claggart believed Squeak's lies. He wanted to believe them. He hated Billy more every day.

'Soon, I'll know something very bad about Budd,' Claggart thought. 'Then I'll punish him. Yes! I will punish him!'

6

The Gold Coins

HMS *Indomitable* was a big ship. But hundreds of men lived on it. The ship was very crowded. The sailors slept in hammocks on the gun-decks. Every night, they fixed their hammocks between the huge guns. The hammocks were very close together.

The weather was very hot in August 1797. One night, Billy got into his hammock and tried to sleep. But he could not sleep. He was hot. There were too many sailors near him. After an hour, Billy went up to the main deck. He lay down on some sails. Another sailor was asleep on the sails nearby.

After half an hour, Billy was still awake. Suddenly, somebody touched his shoulder. Then somebody spoke to him, very quietly.

'Billy!' said the voice. 'Billy Budd! I want to talk to you. Don't say anything. Listen to me!'

The man had a thin, squeaky voice. Billy did not know the voice.

Billy sat up slowly. The night was very dark. Clouds were covering the moon. Billy saw somebody next to him. But he could not see the man's face clearly.

'Who are you? What do you want?' Billy asked.

The man spoke again.

'Listen, Billy,' he said. 'You are an impressed man. I am an impressed man too. There are lots of impressed men on this ship. You are our friend. You can help us, Billy.'

'I don't understand you,' said Billy.

'Don't speak so loudly,' the other man said. 'Help us, Billy. Help us. We must have a strong leader. Will you be our leader? We will give you this!'

The man opened his hand. At that moment, the moon came from behind a cloud. The light from the moon fell on the man's hand. Billy saw some bright, shiny, gold coins in the man's open hand.

Billy was very angry. He wanted to speak but he could not. Then he began to stutter.

'G–g–g–go away!' Billy said. 'T–t–t–take y–y–y–your m–m–money with you! I d–d–don't want your m–m–money and I d–d–don't w–w–want any tr–tr–tr–trouble!'

Billy started to get up and the other man quickly ran away. The sleeping sailor next to Billy woke up.

'What's wrong, Billy?' the other man asked.

'I c–c–caught a thief,' Billy replied angrily. 'I w–w–was s–s–sending him away!'

'Well done, Billy,' said the sailor. 'Well done!' And a few moments later, he was asleep again.

But Billy could not sleep. He thought about the gold coins. Why had the man tried to give him money? Where had the money come from? Billy did not know.

'That man was making trouble,' he said to himself. 'And he was trying to make trouble for me. I must find out about him. Who is the man with the thin, squeaky voice?'

The next day, Billy heard the thin, squeaky voice again. It was the voice of one of the gunners! The man smiled at Billy. And the day after that, the man spoke to Billy. Billy did not reply.

The young foretopman was worried. He talked to Dansker about it. He told Dansker about the man with the squeaky voice.

'What did I tell you?' Dansker said. 'Claggart doesn't like you, Billy. That man was one of his spies. We call him Squeak. You have a powerful enemy on this ship, Billy Budd. And that enemy is John Claggart!'

The old man looked at Billy sadly, and he walked away.

———

Billy had the body of a strong young man. But he had the mind of a child. Billy was good, and he did not understand wicked people.

'Dansker is wrong!' he said to himself. 'I don't have any enemies on this ship.'

Every day, Billy worked harder. He quickly obeyed the officer's orders. He smiled at his friends.

John Claggart saw Billy and he smiled too. But Claggart's smiles were cruel. A cat sees a mouse and it is happy. In the same way, the master-at-arms was happy to see Billy.

'Soon, the cat will catch the mouse,' Claggart said to himself. 'Then, the mouse will die, Billy Budd. The mouse will die!'

7
Who Is the Enemy?

A few days later, *HMS Indomitable* left the Mediterranean Sea. The warship sailed back towards the Channel. It sailed past Gibraltar. After that, Captain Vere asked the lookouts to watch for French ships.

'France is our enemy,' said Vere. 'We will fight her ships. We will send the French ships to the bottom of the sea!'

The lookouts sat at the tops of the tall masts. Soon one of them saw a French ship, near the coast of Spain.

The lookout shouted down to the captain. Vere was standing on the poop deck. Soon, he saw the enemy ship too.

Captain Vere gave orders to his officers.

'Follow that French ship!' he said. 'The gunners must go to their guns. Call all the other men to the main deck. We will chase the enemy ship and we will capture it!'

The crew pulled more sails onto the warship's tall masts. The wind filled the huge sails. The *Indomitable* was moving fast. But the French ship was smaller and faster than *HMS Indomitable*. The big warship could not catch it. Captain Vere chased the enemy ship for many hours, but it escaped.

Captain Vere was angry. He walked around the poop deck. He looked at the empty sea.

Suddenly, the master-at-arms came onto the poop deck.

'What do you want, Mr Claggart?' Vere asked him.

'I have some bad news, Captain,' Claggart replied.

Captain Vere looked at the master-at-arms angrily.

'The French ship escaped,' he said. '*That* is bad news, Mr Claggart!'

'Yes, Captain,' said Claggart. 'The French ship escaped. Some of our men were not working hard enough.'

'I understand you, Master-at-arms,' Vere said quickly. 'You are talking about the impressed men.'

'Yes, sir,' replied Claggart. 'These men have a leader now. You remember the mutinies, sir. Impressed men started those mutinies. Impressed men with clever leaders started them!'

'Why are you talking about the mutinies, Mr Claggart?' Captain Vere asked angrily. 'What are you saying?'

'I am saying this, sir,' replied the master-at-arms. 'There were mutinies in the spring. On one ship, the captain was in great danger. Everybody hates the name of that ship now! We do not want everybody to hate —'

37

'Stop! You have said enough, Master-at-arms,' said Vere. Then he was silent for a minute.

'Claggart works hard,' Vere thought. 'But do I trust him? He's a good sailor. But is he a good man? I don't know. But I must find out the truth!'

Then the captain spoke again.

'There is a dangerous man on my ship?' Vere asked. 'He is planning a mutiny? Are you telling me that, Mr Claggart?'

'Yes, sir. I am telling you that,' replied Claggart.

'And what is the man's name, Master-at-arms?' Vere asked.

'He is William Budd, sir,' Claggart replied quietly. 'William Budd, foretopman. A handsome face can hide a wicked mind, sir.'

Captain Vere was surprised and unhappy. He liked Billy Budd. Budd was a strong young man and a good worker.

'But is Budd wicked? Is he planning a mutiny?' Vere asked himself. 'I cannot believe that. Why is Claggart lying to me?'

'These are dangerous words, Master-at-arms,' said the captain. 'Be very careful. We are at war. Lies are dangerous in a time of war. People are hanged for lies in a time of war. Sailors are hanged from yardarms! I don't want lies, Mr Claggart. I want the truth!'

'I have told you the truth, sir,' said Claggart.

'Then tell me the rest of your story, Mr Claggart,' said the captain sadly.

Carefully, the master-at-arms told his story. Claggart told many lies about William Budd. In his story, Billy became a traitor. Billy's goodbye to his friends on the trading-ship became treason. Billy's words to his friends on the *Indomitable* became treason. In Claggart's story, the honest young sailor was planning a mutiny. Billy wanted a mutiny on the *Indomitable*.

Captain Vere thought about Claggart's story. Did he believe it? He did not know. But he did not want trouble on his ship. The captain turned away from the master-at-arms and he looked at the empty sea. He thought carefully for a few minutes.

'Nobody must know about this,' Vere said to himself. 'I will talk to Billy Budd. But first, the master-at-arms must tell that young man his story. I will watch Budd's face. Then Billy will tell *his* story, and I will listen to it. I will listen to the two men, and I will know the truth.'

Vere turned towards Claggart. The captain had made a decision.

'Call Albert, please, Mr Claggart,' said Vere.

Albert was the captain's own servant. He only worked for the captain. He did not talk with the other sailors. And Vere trusted Albert.

In a few moments, Albert was standing beside his captain.

'Do you know William Budd, the foretopman?' Vere asked the servant.

'Budd, sir? Yes, I know him, sir,' Albert replied.

'Find him for me,' said Vere. 'Bring him to my cabin. Don't answer any of his questions. Go now. Be quick!'

8

Billy Cannot Speak

Three people were standing in Captain Vere's cabin. The door was closed. Albert was standing outside it.

Billy Budd looked at the captain. Then he looked at the master-at-arms. What was going to happen? He did not know, but he was not frightened.

Billy smiled happily.

'The captain likes my work,' he said to himself. 'And he is going to tell the master-at-arms about it.'

Billy smiled. But John Claggart did not smile. And Captain Vere did not smile.

'Tell Budd your story, Mr Claggart,' said Captain Vere.

The master-at-arms stood in front of Billy. He looked into the young foretopman's blue eyes. He began to speak.

Billy listened, but at first he did not understand. Claggart was telling terrible lies about him. Then suddenly, he *did* understand. Dansker had been right. Claggart was his enemy!

Billy's face became pale. His blue eyes opened very wide. But he said nothing. He could not speak!

'Say something, Budd!' Captain Vere said. 'Is Mr Claggart's story true? Speak! Is this the truth?'

Billy was trying to answer. His head was moving. His mouth was open, but no sound came from it.

Captain Vere understood Billy's problem. He was very sorry for the young foretopman. The captain put his hand on Billy's shoulder.

But the captain's words did not help Billy. Again and again, the young man tried to speak. But he could not say anything. He was very angry.

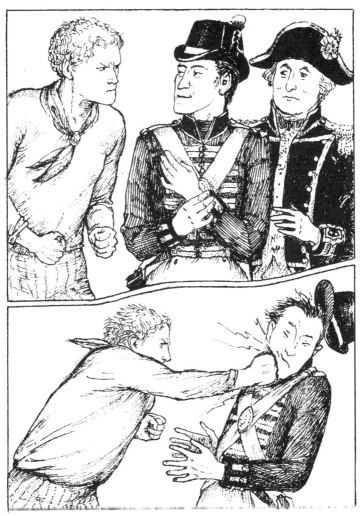

Billy hit the master-at-arms.
Claggart fell to the floor.

The master-at-arms moved once. Then he was still.

'Oh, Billy Budd, Billy Budd, what have you done?' Captain Vere said quietly. 'What have you done?'

The captain and Billy tried to move Claggart. The master-at-arms was very heavy. They tried to wake him, but they could not. Was he dead?

For a few moments, Vere stood without speaking. He covered his face with his hands. Then he pointed to the door of another cabin – his sleeping cabin. He gave an order.

'Go in there, Budd,' he said. 'Stay there. I will call you later.'

Billy obeyed the captain's order. Vere called his servant, Albert.

'Bring the ship's doctor here,' the captain said. 'Then wait outside the cabin again. Go quickly!'

Soon the doctor was in the captain's cabin. He was looking down at the master-at-arms. Blood was coming from Claggart's nose and ears.

'Is he dead, Doctor?' Vere asked.

The doctor looked at Claggart carefully. After a minute, he spoke.

'Yes, Captain,' he said. 'John Claggart is dead.'

The captain's face was very pale.

'A wicked man is dead,' he said quietly. 'And now a good man must die. Yes, a good man must be hanged.'

The doctor did not understand.

'How did Mr Claggart die?' he asked the captain. 'What happened?'

The captain did not answer the doctor's question.

'There must be a trial immediately,' Vere said sadly.

'But how did Claggart die?' the doctor asked again.
'Did somebody kill him? I don't understand.'

'Claggart was a wicked man – a very wicked man,' said Vere. 'He told me lies about William Budd, a young foretopman. In Claggart's story, Billy Budd was planning a mutiny.'

'A mutiny? Budd? I don't believe it,' said the doctor. 'I know Budd. He is a good sailor and a good man.'

'I agree with you, Doctor,' said Vere. 'I sent for Budd. He came to this cabin. I wanted Billy to hear Claggart's story. Then I wanted Billy to tell me the truth.'

'But William Budd has a bad stutter,' the captain said. 'He heard Claggart's story. He became very upset and angry. But he couldn't speak. He wanted to speak. He *tried* to speak. But he *couldn't* speak. He couldn't tell me the truth. He hit the master-at-arms. He killed him. Now there must be a trial.'

'Claggart wanted Billy to be hanged,' said Vere. 'And now Budd *must* be hanged. He must be hanged from the yardarm tomorrow!'

'No, Captain!' said the doctor. 'You must tell Admiral Nelson about this. You must send Budd to the admiral's ship. The trial must happen on the admiral's ship.'

'No, Doctor,' said Captain Vere. 'We cannot wait. We are at war. Budd killed an officer. That is mutiny! There must be a trial now, today! We must not wait. The trial will be here on the *Indomitable*. Please tell my officers, Doctor. Send them to me here.'

The doctor left the cabin.

'Captain Vere is wrong,' he said to himself. 'The admiral must give the order for the trial. Why is the captain doing this? I don't know. But I must obey his order. I will find the officers.'

———

Captain Vere sat alone in his cabin. He had made a difficult decision – a terrible decision!

'The mutinies happened a few months ago,' he thought. 'All the sailors remember the mutinies. There are many impressed men on this ship. We must not have a mutiny on the *Indomitable*.'

'I must be strong,' the captain thought. 'Then the crew will obey my orders. There will be no mutiny. Budd hit an officer and killed him. Budd must die too!'

'I am very sorry for Billy Budd,' thought Captain Vere, sadly. 'But I cannot save him. I must be strong, and he must be strong too.'

9

The Trial

Billy Budd's trial happened in Captain Vere's cabin. Lieutenant Ratcliffe and two other officers were the judges. They had to make a decision. What was the truth about Claggart's death?

Billy stood in front of the three officers. Vere was not a judge – he was a witness.

'I was the only witness to Mr Claggart's death,' Vere told the officers. 'I saw Budd kill the master-at-arms. I will tell you everything.'

The officers listened to the captain's story. They were very surprised.

Lieutenant Ratcliffe spoke to Billy.

'William Budd, you have heard your captain's story,' he said. 'Is his story the truth or not?'

'Captain Vere's story is true,' replied Billy. 'But Mr Claggart's story was *not* true! The master-at-arms told lies about me. I'm not a traitor! I love the King. I love my country!'

'I believe you, Budd,' said Captain Vere.

'Thank you, sir,' Billy replied. 'You are a good man. God bless you!' And his blue eyes filled with tears.

Then one of the other officers asked a question.

'William Budd,' he said. 'Did you hate John Claggart – the master-at-arms?'

'No, sir,' Billy replied. 'I didn't hate him. I'm very sorry about his death. I didn't want to kill him. But he told terrible lies about me. He told lies to my captain. I wanted to answer, but I couldn't speak. So I hit Mr Claggart. That was my answer! My hand became my voice!'

The lieutenant spoke again.

'Did you ever hear about any – any *trouble* on this ship, Budd?' Ratcliffe did not want to say the word 'mutiny'.

Billy thought about Squeak, Claggart's spy. But what had Squeak told him? Nothing. And Billy did not want to make trouble.

'N–n–no, sir!' he said. 'No trouble.'

'Then I have one more question,' said Lieutenant Ratcliffe. 'Why did the master-at-arms tell these lies about you? Can you tell us that?'

Billy shook his head. He could not speak.

'Nobody can answer that question now,' Captain Vere said quickly. 'John Claggart is dead. And William Budd killed him!'

'That is true sir,' said Ratcliffe. 'William Budd, do you want to speak again?'

Billy looked at his captain. But Vere did not speak.

'No, sir,' said Billy sadly.

Captain Vere called his servant. Albert entered the cabin. Vere pointed at the door of his sleeping-cabin.

'William Budd is now a prisoner,' he said. 'Take him into that cabin. Stay with him.'

Albert and Billy went into Captain Vere's sleeping-cabin. Albert closed the door. The three judges looked at each other. Captain Vere turned away from them. He looked out of the cabin window at the empty sea. The sky was light, but the sea was very dark.

After a minute, the three officers started to talk quietly. Captain Vere walked round and round the cabin. At last, he stopped in front of the judges.

'I must say something to you,' Vere said. 'I am not a judge in this trial. I am a witness. This is a difficult trial. Your decision will be difficult. You must all think clearly. Claggart was a wicked man. I know that. He told lies about a good man. We are all sorry for William Budd. I know that too.'

'But our country is at war,' said the captain. 'And we are on one of the King's warships. We must obey the King's law. Budd killed an officer. So Budd must die!'

'But Claggart's death was an accident, sir,' said Lieutenant Ratcliffe. 'It was a terrible accident! Budd did not want to kill the master-at-arms. And he was not planning a mutiny.'

'I agree with you, Lieutenant Ratcliffe,' said Vere. 'But the law is clear. Budd must be hanged.'

Another of the judges spoke.

'Budd did something wrong, sir,' he said. 'But can't we save his life? He is a good man and a good sailor. All the men like him. And they all hated Claggart. They will be angry about Billy's death.'

'We *must* save Budd's life, sir!' said Ratcliffe.

'We are at war,' Captain Vere said again. 'William Budd hit an officer and the man died. That is murder. And it is mutiny too! Budd was an impressed man. There are many impressed men on the *Indomitable*. Some of them were in the mutinies in the spring. They must obey our orders. There must be no more mutinies.'

'Can't we save Budd's life, sir?' asked one of the officers sadly.

'Yes, we can save Budd's life,' said Vere. 'But the men will not understand. They will say, "The officers are weak. The captain is weak." There will be another mutiny! And that must not happen.'

Captain Vere started to walk round the cabin again.

After a moment, Ratcliffe spoke to the other judges.

'Captain Vere is right,' he said quietly. 'There must be no more mutinies. William Budd must die. Do you both agree?'

The other two officers nodded their heads. 'We agree,' they said.

'Sir, we agree with you,' said Lieutenant Ratcliffe. 'William Budd must be hanged.'

'Thank you, gentlemen,' said Captain Vere. 'Budd will be hanged from the yardarm. He will be hanged tomorrow, at dawn. I will tell him your decision.'

———

Captain Vere talked to Billy alone. The two men talked for a long time. What did they say to each other? Nobody ever knew. Vere never told anybody about it. But Albert saw him leaving his cabin. There was a terrible sadness on the captain's face.

Then Albert went into the cabin. And Billy's handsome face was peaceful. The young man was not angry. And he was not frightened.

10

The Death of Billy Budd

Everywhere on the warship, the sailors were talking.

'Where is Billy Budd?' they asked each other. 'And where is the master-at-arms?'

'They both went into the captain's cabin,' one man said. 'But they didn't come out. Is Billy in trouble?'

'Billy in trouble?' another man said. 'No! Billy Budd never does anything wrong. And Captain Vere likes him. Billy isn't in trouble.'

It was late evening. The sea was calm. The moon was shining in the dark sky.

Suddenly, the officers were shouting orders and blowing their whistles.

'All men on deck!' they shouted. 'All men on deck! The captain is going to speak to the crew.'

The men were very surprised. It was late. Why did the captain want to speak to them now?

The men ran to the main deck. Then they stood very still. In the moonlight, their shadows were black on the white deck.

Captain Vere was standing on the poop deck. His officers were standing behind him. And the corporals – Claggart's policemen – were standing near the officers.

There was silence for a moment. Then Vere spoke.

'The master-at-arms is dead,' he said.

The sailors started to speak to each other.

'Silence!' shouted Lieutenant Ratcliffe.

'Mr Claggart's funeral will happen at midnight,' said Captain Vere. 'You will all watch the funeral.'

'William Budd, foretopman, hit Mr Claggart and killed him,' said Vere. 'The King's law is clear. William Budd killed an officer. That is murder and it is mutiny. The punishment for murder and mutiny is death! William Budd will be hanged from the yardarm. He will be hanged at dawn. You will all watch the punishment.'

The men turned towards each other and started to speak again. They were angry.

'Silence!' shouted Lieutenant Ratcliffe. 'Return to your work. Return to your decks. Go immediately!'

An hour later, the officers called the crew to the main deck again. Everybody watched John Claggart's funeral.

The captain of *HMS Indomitable* spoke for a short time.

After that, Claggart's body dropped down into the deep water.

———

Billy was on the lower gun-deck. He was lying on the floor. But Billy was lying in the dark shadow between two of the guns. There were chains on his hands and feet. He could not move. Two guards stood near him.

Billy did not move and he did not speak. His face was very peaceful. The young sailor's life was finished. He was going to die. But he was not frightened.

The hours passed.

At last, dawn came. Billy's last night was ending and his last day was beginning. He heard the corporals coming towards him.

———

The officers blew their whistles. Sailors ran onto the main deck. They came from every part of the ship. After a minute, they were all standing together near the fore mast. They were going to watch their friend die.

Then they heard the sound of the drums. Six men in red uniforms – marines – came onto the deck. They were playing long drums. The sound was terrible.

The ship's officers stood on the poop deck. Some of the corporals stood beside them.

Two more corporals brought Billy onto the deck. He stood under a yardarm of the fore mast. The corporals tied the young sailor's hands together with rope. Then they tied his feet together.

A sailor climbed up to the yardarm. He put a long rope over it. The two ends hung down to the deck. The corporals tied one end of the rope round Billy's neck. Two sailors on the deck held the other end. Everything was ready!

Billy turned and looked at his captain. He spoke clearly.

'God bless you, Captain Vere,' he said.

Everybody was surprised. And suddenly, all the sailors shouted.

'God bless you, Captain Vere!'

Vere stood very still. Then he moved his hand quickly.

The two sailors pulled the rope. They pulled Billy Budd up from the deck, up to the yardarm. The rope was tight round Billy's neck. He could not breathe. In a moment, he was dead.

Billy Budd died. And at that moment, the sun shone for the first time that day. The sun's light shone on the young sailor's body. In the sunlight, the body moved slowly from side to side.

At first, nobody spoke. Nobody moved. The sea made the only sound. Then another sound came from all the sailors. It was an angry sound and it became louder and louder!

11

Captain Vere's Last Battle

Quickly, Captain Vere gave an order. The officers blew their whistles. The corporals moved towards the sailors on the main deck. For a moment, the sailors stood still. Then they moved and returned to their work. Soon, everybody on the *Indomitable* was busy.

Two of Billy's friends brought his body down from the yardarm. They put it carefully on the deck. Then they put the body in a piece of sail. They tied ropes round it and they tied some heavy pieces of metal to it.

Later, the officers called the *Indomitable's* crew back to the main deck. All the men stood together, silently. They watched Billy's funeral. They watched his body drop into the sea.

Suddenly, some big white sea-birds flew close to the ship. They made strange, sad noises. They were the singers at Billy's funeral.

The sun was shining brightly in the clear blue sky. The ship sailed on.

HMS *Indomitable* sailed on. Soon, the lookouts saw a French ship. Captain Vere gave orders to his crew. The *Indomitable* chased the French warship. After half an hour, the two ships were very close together. Both ships fired their guns. At last, the men of the *Indomitable* were fighting in a battle.

All the sailors fought bravely. But a French bullet hit Captain Vere. He was badly injured.

The Indomitable won the battle. The British crew captured the French ship. They took the ship back to Gibraltar. And they took Captain Vere to the hospital there. He lived for a few days and then he died quietly. Vere's last words were, 'Billy Budd, Billy Budd.'

Published by Macmillan Heinemann ELT
Between Towns Road, Oxford OX4 3PP
Macmillan Heinemann ELT is an imprint of
Macmillan Publishers Limited
Companies and representatives throughout the world
Heinemann is a registered trademark of Harcourt Education, used under licence.

ISBN 978–1–4050–7227–4

This retold version by Margaret Tarner for Macmillan Readers
First published 1999
Text © Margaret Tarner 1999, 2002, 2005
Design and illustration © Macmillan Publishers Limited 1999, 2002, 2005

This edition first published 2005

Illustrated by Annabel Large
Map on page 3 by Peter Harper
Illustrations on page 5 and 6 by Patrick Williams
Original cover template design by Jackie Hill
Cover photography by Corbis
Acknowledgements: The publishers would like to thank Mary Evans
Picture Library for permission to reproduce the picture on page 4.

Printed in Thailand

2011 2010 2009 2008 2007
10   9   8   7   6   5   4   3